P9-CJV-536

Herbert Hoover

Herbert Hoover

Martha E. Kendall

AMERICA'S 31ST PRESIDENT

Children's Press®
A Division of Scholastic Inc.
New York / Toronto / London / Auckland / Sydney
Mexico City / New Delhi / Hong Kong
Danbury, Connecticut

Library of Congress Cataloging-in-Publication Data

Kendall, Martha E., 1947–
Herbert Hoover / by Martha E. Kendall.
p. cm.—(Encyclopedia of presidents. Second series)
Includes bibliographical references and index.
ISBN 0-516-22963-X
1. Hoover, Herbert, 1874–1964—Juvenile literature. 2. Presidents—United States—Biography—Juvenile literature. [1. Hoover, Herbert, 1874–1964. 2. Presidents.] I. Title. II. Series.
E802.K46 2004
973.91'6'092—dc22 2003027247

 Published in 2004 by Children's Press, an imprint of Scholastic Library Publishing. Published simultaneously in Canada.
Printed in the United States of America.

1 2 3 4 5 6 7 8 9 10 R 13 12 11 10 09 08 07 06 05 04

Contents

Chapter 1

On His Own and On the Move

Orphan of the Heartland

Herbert Clark Hoover was born in a small three-room house in West Branch, Iowa, on August 10, 1874. He was the second of Jesse and Hulda Hoover's three children. His brother Theodore was three years older, and his sister Mary would be two years younger. West Branch was a prairie town of about 200 people. The Hoovers were members of the Society of Friends (Quakers), a Christian group well known for its simple form of worship and its opposition to war.

Herbert, soon nicknamed "Bertie," grew up in a strict family that did not allow card playing, the reading of fiction (which they considered "untruth"), or any alcohol in their home. Twice a week the family attended "Quaker meeting," where even children were required to sit quietly during services that could last two hours. He later recalled the experience as "strong training in patience" when he sat silently and so still that he "might not even count his toes."

Herbert Hoover's birthplace in West Branch, Iowa.

In the summer, Hoover's family picnicked on the banks of the Cedar River. Hoover and his friends fished, using "willow poles with a butcher-string line and hooks ten for a dime." They ate their catch of sunfish and catfish after cooking it over an open fire. In the winter, the boys went sledding on snow-covered Cook's Hill near his home.

Jesse Hoover was a blacksmith, skilled at making horseshoes and farm implements by shaping red-hot metal. One day, young Bertie stepped on a red-hot iron chip and suffered a painful burn. The injury left a scar that he later called his "brand from Iowa." Jesse Hoover's business prospered, and he opened a farm implements store, but when Bertie Hoover was six years old, his father died suddenly of heart disease. Hulda Hoover was left with the difficult job of supporting three children. She served as a minister in the Society of Friends, rented out a room in the Hoovers' small house, and took in sewing. Her work as a minister required her to travel often, and she left her children with other Quaker families in West Branch. Even with all her effort, the family barely managed.

The children were sent to live for weeks or months with relatives to ease the financial burden. Hoover spent a few months with an uncle, Laban Miles, in Indian Territory, where Miles was an Indian agent on a reservation for the Osage tribe. The Native American boys taught Hoover how to make bows and arrows.

Only three years after the death of her husband, Hulda Hoover came down with typhoid fever. Weakened by the disease, she developed pneumonia and died, leaving the Hoover children orphans. Tad was about 12, Bertie was 9, and May was 7. There was no family member or neighbor able to support all three children. Years later, Hoover wrote, "After her death, our home was necessarily broken up." Each of the children was sent to live with different relatives. Hoover was

Jesse and Hulda Hoover, Herbert's parents. They both died before he was ten years old, leaving three children as orphans.

taken in by his Uncle Allen and Aunt Millie Hoover and their son, who lived on a farm a mile from West Branch. Although the family was kind to him, Hoover lay awake at night, missing his mother. She had taught him that if he had nothing good to say, to say nothing at all. Enduring his loneliness without complaint, he withdrew into himself. Then, two years later, he faced yet another separation.

At the age of eleven, Hoover left West Branch for good. In 1885, he was sent to live with an uncle and aunt, John and Laura Minthorn, in Oregon. He boarded a train all by himself for the long journey across the country. Soon after he arrived, he wrote a letter to his first grade teacher in West Branch. He said he was disappointed to discover that the Rocky Mountains were in fact "mostly made of dirt."

John and Laura Minthorn ran the Friends Pacific Academy, a small Quaker school in Newberg, about 20 miles (32 kilometers) from Portland.

Hoover's Autograph

The earliest autograph of Hoover appears in a classmate's autograph book after this rhyme:

> Let your days be days of peas,
> Slip along as slick as greese.

(He may have meant to write "days of peace" and "slick as grease.")

Hoover enrolled at the school, where he was expected to be serious in his studies. He also was expected to work hard at the Minthorns' house. He fed and watered their horses, brought the cows in from the pasture and milked them, and split wood for the fireplace.

When John Minthorn decided to clear a section of fir forest, he assigned Hoover the chore of burning the felled trees, some of which measured 4 feet (1.2 meters) across. Hoover later described the process: "This was done by boring two holes in the stump of the logs at such angles that they would meet at about a foot deep. Into the top hole we pushed burning charcoal and by blowing in the lower hole would start an internal fire." After the first few times, he wrote, "I came to look upon a fir tree as a public enemy."

A medical doctor as well as a teacher, Minthorn sometimes asked Hoover to accompany him on long drives to call on patients in the countryside. Minthorn took a personal interest in young Herbert, urging him to take an active role in life. "The worst thing a man can do is to do nothing," he said. Hoover remembered his uncle's advice, but he was usually quiet and subdued. No doubt he missed his parents, his sister and brother, and his Iowa home.

In 1888 Hoover helped his uncle set up the Oregon Land Company in Salem, the state capital. One evening he overheard his uncle arguing with a group

The Hoover children in 1888: Theodore, Mary, and Herbert. After their mother died in 1884, they were split up and raised by different families.

of men who had come to collect a debt. Hoover sensed from the rising voices that the situation could become violent. Then suddenly, the lights went out. The frustrated men groped their way home in the dark. Meeting again the next day, after a good night's sleep, they reached an agreement. What had happened to the electricity? Hoover himself had shut it off.

The Pioneer

In 1890, when Hoover was 16, he saw a newspaper notice about a new university in California. The school, Stanford University, in Palo Alto, was scheduled to open in 1891. A recruiter visited Hoover and encouraged him to enroll in the school's first class. There was no tuition fee. Hoover had considered other colleges, but Stanford was his first choice because it would be offering courses in engineering, the subject he most wanted to study.

First, he had to pass the entrance examinations. He soon found that he didn't have the skills and knowledge, failing all the exams except mathematics. The recruiter was so impressed by Hoover's determination, however, that he invited him to come to Palo Alto to be tutored. Hoover later wrote, "I gathered up all my possessions—being $160 of savings, two suits of clothes and a bicycle. . . . The Minthorn family added $50 and put me on the train with blessings, affections—and food." After a summer of tutoring, Hoover took the exams again and scored well enough to be admitted to the university. He moved into the men's dormitory even before the university began operations. He liked to say that this made him "the first student at Stanford."

Hoover selected mechanical engineering as his major. Even though there was no tuition payment, he had to work hard to pay for his room and board. He worked as a clerk, ran a laundry, delivered newspapers, and managed special lectures and concerts. After the first year, he had discovered that he liked *geology* (the study of the earth and its formation) even better than engineering, and changed his major. In the summers, his geology professor,

Stanford University, where Hoover graduated in 1895. For many years, he considered the university town of Palo Alto his home, but he rarely spent much time there.

Dr. John Caspar Branner, arranged for him to work on geological surveys of Arkansas and of California's Sierra Nevada mountains. The jobs earned him about $40 a month.

Even with all his part-time jobs, Hoover found time to participate in campus events. He helped lead a protest against the way student organizations accounted for their money and was elected treasurer of the student activities fund. He found that the fund was deep in debt and soon worked out a plan to increase its income and limit its expenditures. He also became the manager of the Stanford baseball and football teams.

Horse and the Centipede

When Hoover helped with a geological study in the Sierra Nevada mountains near Lake Tahoe, he loved the terrain but hated the transportation, a horse. He wrote, "In these long mountain rides over trails and through the brush, I arrived finally at the conclusion that a horse was one of the original mistakes of creation. I felt he was too high off the ground for convenience and safety on mountain trails. He would have been better if he had been given a dozen legs so that he had the smooth and sure pace of a centipede. Furthermore he should have had scales as protection against flies, and a larger water-tank like a camel."

The Stanford surveying team in 1893. Hoover is at lower left.

Hoover's Bride

Lou Henry was the first woman to graduate with a geology degree from Stanford. Here she takes a comical pose on the porch of her sorority house.

Lou Henry was born March 29, 1874, to a Quaker family in Waterloo, Iowa. After they met at Stanford, Hoover and Henry discovered they were born within six months of each other in towns only about 100 miles (160 km) apart. When she was ten, Lou Henry moved with her family to southern California, where they eventually settled in Whittier, a town established by Quaker settlers from the Midwest.

From earliest childhood, Lou Henry loved the outdoors. Her father took her fishing, camping, hiking, and horseback riding. In California, she organized her playmates to clear 5 acres (2 hectares) to make a baseball diamond. When some volunteers said they were scared of the bugs, she told them, "Never mind the spiders. They won't hurt you."

When Lou was 16, her family moved to Monterey, California, where her father opened a bank. During the summer of 1894, Lou attended a science class in Pacific Grove, near Monterey. It was taught by Hoover's geology professor, Dr. Branner. According to biographer Helen Pryor, Lou said, "I love the out-of-doors and want to know how the world is made and that is what I'll learn in geology." She enrolled at Stanford, where she became the only woman in her class to study geology and mining.

During his senior year, Hoover continued to love the study of geology. He also fell in love with Lou Henry, a first-year student. But work came before romance.

Going for the Gold

After Hoover graduated from Stanford in 1895, he returned to the Sierra Nevada mountains for another summer of geological fieldwork. When fall came, an economic slowdown made jobs scarce. He finally found work at the Reward Gold Mine in Grass Valley, California. He pushed an ore car through the lower levels of the mine for ten hours each night and earned $14 a week. There he learned the harsh reality of being a miner. When the mine cut back on its workforce, Hoover found another mining job nearby, but he was determined to find a job above the ground. He soon took a position with a mining firm directed by Louis Janin in San Francisco. He began doing clerical jobs, but then was assigned to geologic fieldwork in Colorado and New Mexico.

In 1897 the British firm Bewick, Moreing and Company announced a position with a salary of $7,200 per year (then a huge amount). The company was looking for a mature man skilled in American mining practices to help develop its gold mines in Western Australia. Even though Hoover was only 23 years old, Janin recommended him for the position.

Herbert Hoover at 23 in London, where he landed a job as an engineer with an international mining firm.

Hoover traveled to London and met the owners of Bewick, Moreing and Company. He soon learned that he was "a tenderfoot" in matters of fashion and upper-class conversation. Even so, he impressed the managers of the firm and got the job. He was assigned to gold mines the company operated in Australia, halfway around the world.

To get to Australia, Hoover crossed the English Channel by boat, then rode for two days and two nights on a slow train from northern France to Italy. There he boarded the RMS *Victoria* for the trip through the Suez Canal and across the Indian Ocean to Australia. Three weeks later, he walked ashore and boarded a train for the remote "outback," where the Bewick, Moreing mines were located. One visitor described the seemingly endless acres of flat land as "wearisome beyond words . . . one dark unbroken sea of trackless bush."

Hoover quickly adapted to the country. He traveled to remote mines by riding a camel, an animal he said was "even a less successful creation than a horse." Hoover slept on the ground under the stars, and sometimes ate little more than bread, cocoa, and sardines. He also proved to be a skilled and effective manager. He recognized the potential of one mine, called the Sons of Gwalia, and urged the company to develop it. Bewick, Moreing invested $500,000 in the mine, and over the next 50 years, it yielded $55 million worth of gold. Soon

Hoover at the mines in Australia.

Hoover was named the consulting engineer for five Australian gold mines. He said, "To feel great works grow under one's feet and to have more men constantly getting good jobs is to be the master of contentment."

As his assignment in Australia came to an end, Hoover was thinking about more than mines and miners. He would soon be working at another remote post, but first he planned to visit California. From Australia, he sent a telegram to Lou Henry, saying, "Will you marry me?" She accepted his proposal. They were married at her parents' home in Monterey, California, on February 10, 1899. The next day, the Hoovers began their honeymoon, a month-long voyage from San Francisco to China. Hoover had accepted a new assignment from Bewick, Moreing, as chief engineer of the Chinese Engineering and Mining Company. Only 24 years old, he had earned an exciting challenge in yet another new country.

Chapter 2 Star-Spangled Hoover

The "Great Engineer"

Hoover arrived in China as the representative of Bewick, Moreing and Company in 1899. His main aim was to manage and increase the company's coal-mining businesses there. At the time, coal was the most necessary of all world fuels, used for making steel, generating electricity, and heating homes and public buildings. Hoover also became an adviser to the Chinese government.

Hoover negotiated agreements for Bewick, Moreing and Company to develop additional mines and set up an American-style system of managing them. He was frustrated by the Chinese custom known as "the squeeze," a form of bribery that required payments to nonexistent employees. He worked patiently to end the custom and succeeded in reducing its effects. Still, legal and political wrangling between Chinese officials and the British company continued.

The Hoovers made a special effort to understand China and the Chinese. Lou Hoover learned to speak and read Mandarin (one of the important languages of China), while Hoover learned a smattering of it. They also studied Chinese customs and etiquette. Hoover came to realize that there would be many misunderstandings and disagreements when people of different cultures work together. Still, he developed an "abiding admiration" for the Chinese people, especially regarding their close family ties, their affection for their children, and their willingness to work hard.

Even before the Hoovers arrived in China, a group of Chinese revolutionaries was beginning a battle against foreign traders and businesses. Known as the Boxers because they practiced the martial arts, they stormed the large cities of northern China. The Chinese government was unwilling or unable to control the Boxers, and in 1900 they attacked neighborhoods where foreigners lived in Tientsin, Peking, and other large cities.

The Hoovers lived outside the part of Tientsin fortified by European governments, and they helped prepare for Boxer attacks, building barricades and organizing food distribution. Soon the neighborhood was surrounded by Boxer attackers and cut off from the outside world. During one attack, five shells blasted the Hoovers' home. The structure was badly damaged, but no one was hurt. The

Lou Hoover poses with a field gun during the siege of Tientsin by the Chinese revolutionaries.

violent siege lasted more than four weeks. Finally, an international force, made up of troops from European countries and the United States, arrived to break the siege and restore communication with the outside world.

In 1901, Hoover was nominated to be one of Bewick, Moreing's junior partners. The Hoovers moved to London. Both of their sons, Herbert Clark Junior and Allan Henry, were born there. From his base in London, Hoover traveled the globe. Between 1902 and 1907, he circled the world five times, sometimes traveling alone, sometimes taking the whole family. When they were in London, they lived in a large old two-story villa that they referred to as their "red house."

The Rescue

During the Boxer Rebellion, a stray shell hit the house of the Tongs, a Chinese family who lived near the Hoovers. The mother of the family and her baby were killed. Hoover rescued the surviving children, carrying them back to his home, where Mrs. Hoover cared for them. The father of the family, Tong Shao-yi, later became the first premier of the Republic of China. His daughter married Wellington Koo, the Chinese ambassador to the United States.

Eighteen years later, Mrs. Koo was introduced to the Hoovers in Washington, D.C. "I have met you before," she said. "I am Tong Shao-yi's daughter whom you carried across the street during the siege of Tientsin."

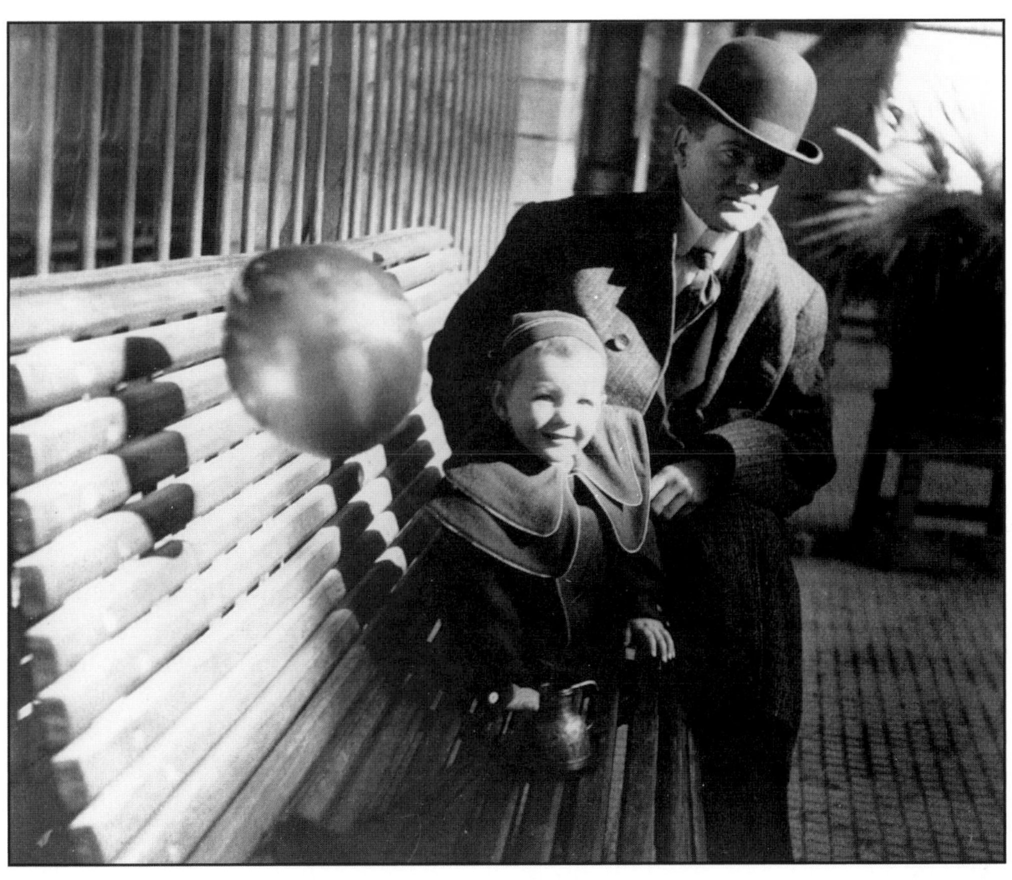

Hoover with his young son Herbert Jr. in a railway station in Cairo, Egypt, during one of the family's many long trips.

The Hoovers felt uncomfortable with the British class system. It was expected, for example, that they not form personal friendships with the men and women who worked in their home as servants. The family paid little attention to expectations. The Hoover boys regularly played with the servants' children, and the family formed lifelong ties of affection with many of their household workers.

The Hoovers entertained a great deal. Mrs. Hoover's gracious, outgoing personality contrasted with her husband's shyness. He rarely looked directly at people during a social conversation, and he was not good at small talk. In fact, after one dinner party, the woman who sat next to Hoover described him as "a grunter"—"I'd say something, and he'd just say 'unh.'"

In London, Herbert and Lou Hoover established a large international circle of friends. In addition, they were using their past experiences to develop new skills and hobbies. One of Hoover's projects was to catalog and standardize international mining laws. Lou Hoover translated the Chinese laws for him. She also helped him organize his first book, *The Principles of Mining*, which became an influential guide to the industry.

The Hoovers collaborated on a scholarly project as well. They agreed to translate a famous book about mining written in the 1500s, *De Re Metallica*. This project was "a labor of love." Hoover wanted to demonstrate that mining science and engineering had played an important role in history. "Science is the base upon which is reared the civilization of today," he wrote. The couple not only wrote the book but paid for it to be printed and gave away most of the 3,000 copies to mining leaders, schools, and interested students.

As Hoover's wealth grew, he was consistently generous. At various times, he offered unexpected vacation bonuses to household employees, provided money to the family of a colleague in trouble, and paid for the education of needy Stanford students. Most of these contributions were made quietly and without publicity. He preferred to work behind the scenes.

In 1907 Hoover visited an abandoned silver mine in Burma (now Myanmar). While exploring its old narrow tunnels by the light of a candle, he was amazed by the richness of the silver and zinc. He quickly ended his exploration when he saw a huge fresh footprint made by a Bengal tiger. Hoover reported the mine's enormous potential and recommended that it be reopened. Engineering problems in the rugged territory plagued the mine for years afterward, but Hoover refused to give up.

Finally he planned construction of a tunnel nearly a mile and a half (2.4 km) long. It ran from the side of the mountain into the mine, making it easier to transport the ore to the surface. The tunnel took 200 men more than three years to build, but when it was completed, the operation proved highly profitable. The mine's success improved the lives of more than 100,000 people in the region. It also helped Hoover increase his personal wealth.

The Wealthy Orphan

By age 34, Herbert Hoover had become a millionaire. He might have continued at Bewick, Moreing and earned many more millions, but he had other concerns. The

Hoovers' older son was about to start school, and his parents wanted their boys to grow up in the United States. Hoover praised the American value of equality of opportunity so often that he was nicknamed "Star-Spangled Hoover" and "Hail Columbia Hoover." In 1909, Hoover resigned from Bewick, Moreing, and his family moved back to California. There he set up an independent consulting business providing advice and assistance to mining companies around the world.

The Hoovers settled in Palo Alto, a stone's throw from Stanford University. Hoover continued to travel. As a world-famous "doctor of sick mines," he helped make dozens of mining operations more profitable and often helped administer them. By 1914, he was a director of 18 mining and financial companies, which employed 100,000 people around the globe.

Hoover did not limit his interests to mining. He read about other subjects for two hours every evening, and during long ocean voyages. He avoided anything resembling a vacation. One time on a picnic with friends, he suggested they build a dam on a nearby stream. Like most of his projects, the effort grew larger and larger until it contained drains, channels, and elevated canals.

At the age of 40, Hoover had more money than he could easily spend, and he told friends that "just making money isn't enough." He hoped to use his skills to benefit his country as a whole. Now that he had made his fortune, he would do just that.

"Food Will Win the War"

In August 1914, war broke out between the countries of Europe, and a powerful German army invaded Belgium. Thousands of Americans who were living or traveling in Europe were caught by surprise. Railroads and ships quit running, and travelers had no way to return home. At that moment, the Hoovers were visiting London. The U.S. Consulate asked Hoover to help American citizens leave war-threatened parts of Europe and return home. Herbert and Lou Hoover both worked for the cause, raising money and organizing transportation that enabled the Americans to flee. When Lou Hoover left England in October to enroll the boys in school in California, Herbert Hoover stayed on. Altogether, the Hoovers' organization served 120,000 American citizens.

Before Hoover could return to the United States, another crisis arose. The people of Belgium, who normally relied on food imported from other countries, were beginning to starve. They were caught between the invading German army, which fed only its own troops, and the British navy, which didn't allow food to be landed in Belgian ports, in order to starve German troops.

With the support of the U.S. ambassador to Britain, Hoover became the director of the Commission for Relief in Belgium. Sometimes working around the clock, he negotiated with the Germans and the British to gain permission to land food for the Belgian people. He raised money to buy food, much of it from the United States, and organized a small navy of ships to deliver it. For more than four years, the commission managed to provide enough food for millions of people in Belgium and northern France, even as the war continued all around them. Hoover refused to take a salary for his work with the commission and refused all offers of honors or recognition. U.S. Ambassador Walter Hines Page praised Hoover in a letter to President Wilson: "He's a simple, modest, energetic man who began his career in California and will end it in Heaven."

In 1917, during the third year of fighting, the United States entered the war on the side of Britain and France against Germany and Austria-Hungary. President Wilson asked Hoover to return to the United States to become U.S. Food Administrator for the war effort. Many in the government argued that the government should pass laws *rationing* food, limiting the amount of basic food items families and individuals could buy. Hoover disagreed. He persuaded the government that a voluntary plan for saving food would be just as effective.

The Food Administration began a huge advertising campaign to persuade the public to eat less so that surplus food could be sent to Europe for Allied troops and civilians. The main theme of the campaign was "Food Will Win the War." Families were urged to observe "Meatless Mondays" and "Wheatless Wednesdays." Reminded by a song, "The Patriotic Potato," homemakers were encouraged to serve potatoes instead of bread. Doing so conserved wheat, which could

A poster urges Americans to conserve to help feed war victims in Europe. Hoover was the moving force in supplying food for Belgian civilians during World War I.

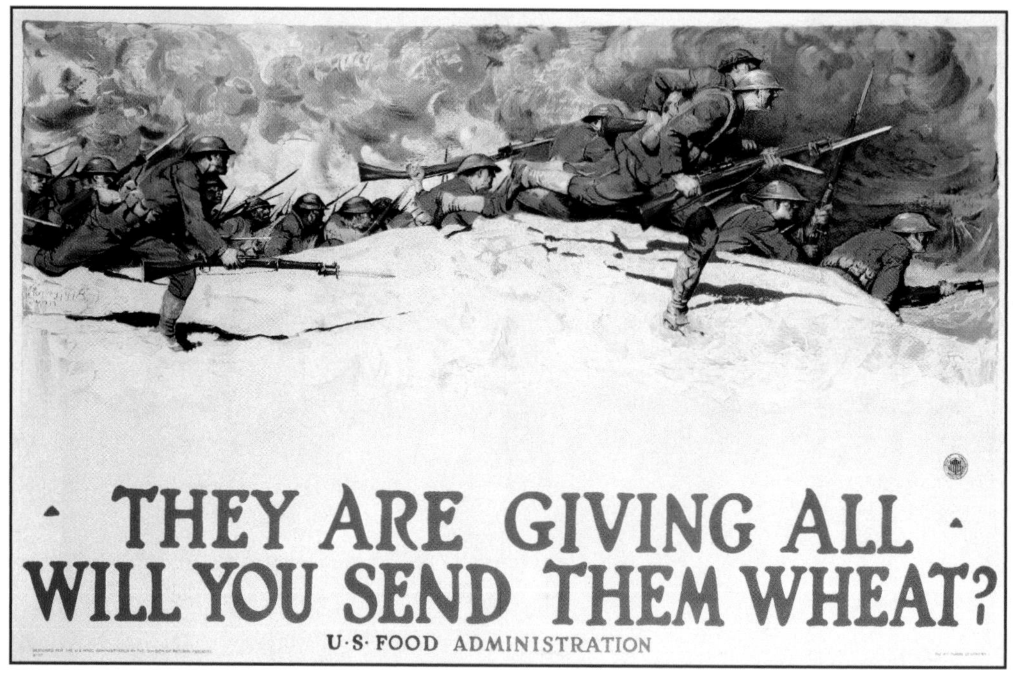

THEY ARE GIVING ALL
WILL YOU SEND THEM WHEAT?
U·S· FOOD ADMINISTRATION

After the United States entered World War I in 1917, Hoover headed the U.S. Food Administration, which shipped food to Allied troops and civilians in Europe.

be shipped overseas. Conserving food came to be known as "Hooverizing." The campaign succeeded in reducing U.S. consumption of food and allowed the huge shipments of food to Europe.

The Great War (now known as World War I) came to an end in November 1918 when the German government asked for an *armistice* (an agreement to stop fighting while a peace treaty is negotiated). Soon afterward, President Woodrow Wilson sent Hoover to Europe to estimate the need for food in countries torn by

"Hooverizing"

A popular Valentine poster during the war years had fun with Hoover's campaign:

I can Hooverize on dinners
and on lights and fuel too,
But I'll never learn to Hooverize
When it comes to loving you!

war. Based in Paris, Hoover took on the enormous task of distributing food and raw materials to civilians in western Europe. He organized more huge shipments of food from the United States to provide nourishment to millions. At first, American allies objected to shipping aid to Germany. Hoover rejected their complaint. "We have never fought with women and children, and our desire must be to see the wounds of war healed through the world," he wrote. Even after the government ended shipments of food to Europe, Hoover set up a private charity called the European Children's Fund, which continued to send food to nourish needy children.

In 1919, Hoover returned to the United States after nearly six years away. He and Lou began construction of an elegant home in Palo Alto, which she had

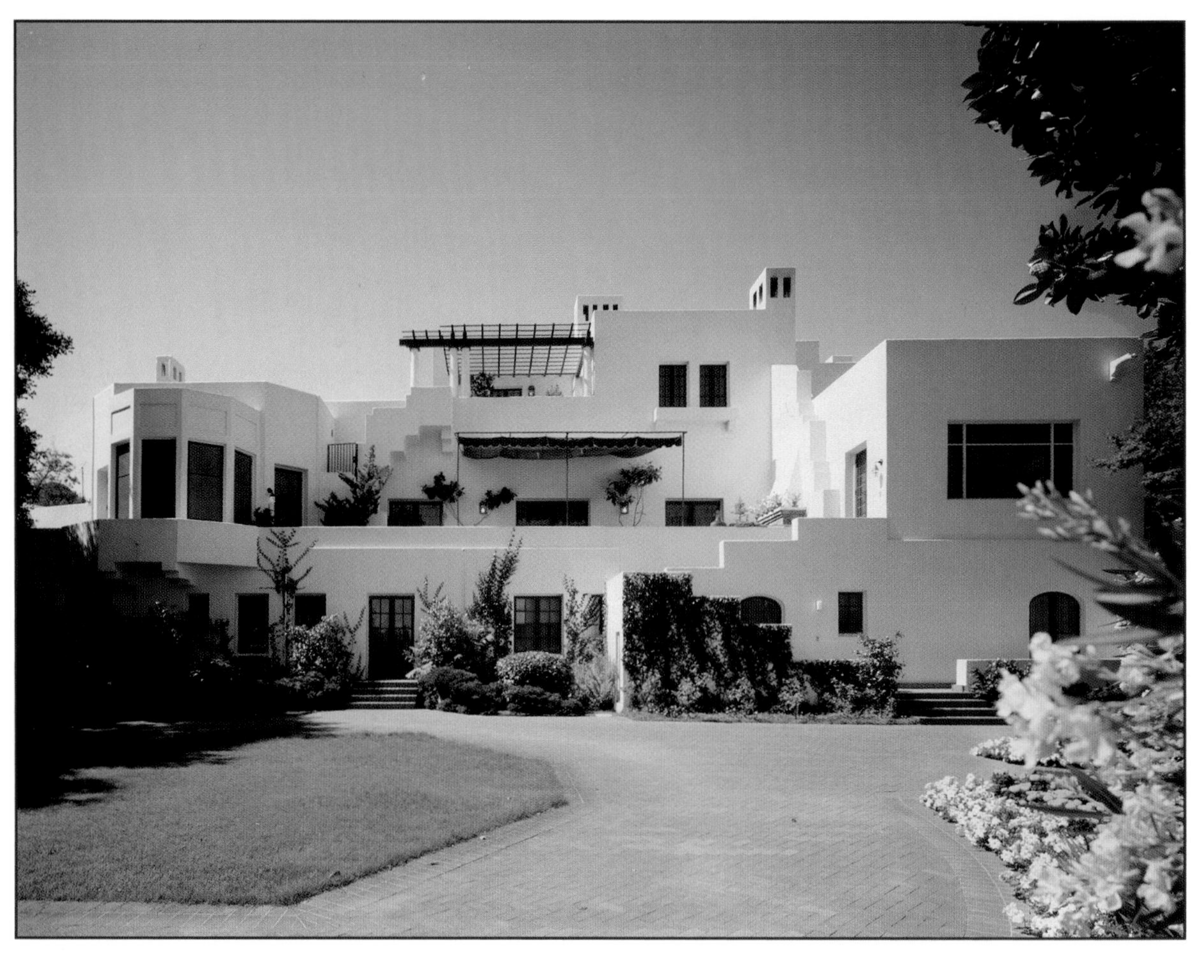

Lou Hoover helped design this palatial house, which the Hoovers built in Palo Alto, California, near the campus of Stanford University.

helped design. His sons hoped that he would remain in California for a long time to come, and he appeared to agree. He told friends that he wanted "to get out of the limelight as far as possible."

His great accomplishment had made him one of America's most admired people, however, and many citizens wondered what he would do next. Political leadership seemed one obvious answer. When asked about a role in the government, Hoover replied, "I do not believe that I have the mental attitude or the politician's manner."

Despite his misgivings, politics refused to leave him alone.

Chapter 3 American Individualism

Labor and Management

In the fall of 1919, the administration of President Wilson was concerned about growing conflicts between American *labor* (those who worked in factories) and *management* (the owners and managers of the factories). Wilson's secretary of labor called a conference including representatives of American industry, labor, and the general public to discuss the problems, but the participants soon fell to arguing, and the conference broke up. Herbert Hoover was asked to serve as vice chairman of a second conference in December. He succeeded largely because of his reputation and skill at mediating. Hoover helped draft the final report and presented its findings in speeches around the country.

The report favored reducing the workday from twelve hours to eight hours, setting a guaranteed minimum wage, prohibiting child labor, and requiring equal pay for men and women. It also supported the rights of labor *unions*. Hoover believed that ideal managers would treat workers fairly, making unions unnecessary. In the real world, however, unions could protect the rights of workers against owners and managers who took advantage of them.

When Hoover presented his report at business gatherings, it often received a cool response. Describing one such presentation to the Boston Chamber of Commerce, he later wrote, "When I sat down from this address, the applause would not have waked a nervous baby."

Hoover had registered as a Republican in the mid-1890s, but he had not been active in party politics. In 1920 he admired President Woodrow Wilson and some other Democrats for their "highest purpose and ideals." Yet he still favored the Republican party because its membership included many whose views he understood and took as his own: "skilled workmen, farmers, professionals and small-business men."

As the 1920 election approached, a group of professors at Harvard University urged Hoover to run for president, believing he could "Hooverize" politics with his idealistic values. Hoover resisted the invitation, although his name did appear on the ballot in the California Republican primary. At the national Republican convention, former senator Warren Harding of Ohio won the presidential nomination. In November, Harding was elected president.

Harding invited Hoover to serve in his cabinet as secretary of agriculture or secretary of commerce. Hoover was interested in the appointment as *secretary of commerce*, but was worried that the post did not give him "a wide enough field." His role would be to encourage U.S. trade both at home and abroad, but the Department of Commerce was small and lacked influence. Hoover told Harding, "To be of real service, I must have a voice on all important economic policies of the administration. . . . business, agriculture, labor, finance, and foreign affairs." Harding agreed, and Hoover accepted the nomination. Once again, Hoover left California. Herbert Jr. stayed there to enroll at Stanford University, but Lou and younger son Allan moved with him to Washington.

"Secretary of Commerce and Under Secretary of Everything Else"

Hoover served as secretary of commerce for more than seven years. He transformed the Department of Commerce from a collection of small agencies to an organization of several thousand employees. His energy and hard work affected other departments of government as well. He became known as "Secretary of Commerce and Under Secretary of everything else." Hoover hated waste and proposed many policies to improve efficiency. He supported making cheap electricity available to greater numbers of people; the conservation of water, oil, and

Secretary of Commerce Hoover and his wife attend a baseball game with President Warren Harding and his wife in 1922.

coal; the streamlining of government; the production of industrial parts in standard sizes so that they could be used interchangeably; the improvement of vehicle safety codes to reduce traffic injuries and deaths; simplifying the regulations affecting new home construction; the improvement of public health care for children; and investment in scientific research.

When any issue arose, Hoover would ask, "What are the facts?" He organized hundreds of fact-finding conferences to bring together people in government and private business. The meetings received much publicity and helped inform Americans about ways they could help solve problems in society. Topics ranged from transportation (the need for new bridges and highways), to illiteracy, to children's health and welfare.

Progressives

Between 1901 and 1920, presidents from both parties—Republicans Theodore Roosevelt and William Howard Taft, and Democrat Woodrow Wilson—identified themselves as "progressives" and implemented a series of reforms. These included strengthening government regulation of business, recognizing the rights of labor and consumers, and conserving government lands.

President Harding and Vice President Coolidge were elected in 1920 on a campaign to return the country to "normalcy." To many in the Republican party, this meant an end to ambitious reforms and a reduction of government power. Herbert Hoover was an exception. Many of the actions he fought for as secretary of commerce continued the progressive policies of earlier days. He respected the rights of business and did not favor "big government," but he was not afraid to speak up for progressive goals.

Empowering Girls and Women

Lou Hoover participated in many voluntary organizations. She became honorary president of the Girl Scouts and helped raise more than $2 million to help increase its membership. There were only 100,000 Girl Scouts in 1921; by 1933, when the Hoovers left the White House, there were more than a million.

Mrs. Hoover also supported women's participation in athletics. In 1923, as the only female officer of the National Amateur Athletic Federation, she organized a women's division to promote increased opportunities for women in amateur sports. She also encouraged many organizations in which women could be active, including the League of Women Voters, parent-teacher associations, and the Young Women's Christian Association (YWCA).

Lou Hoover continued her busy schedule of volunteer work as first lady.

In 1922, Hoover published a booklet called "American Individualism." It discussed many "-isms," including communism, socialism, and capitalism. Finally it described "American individualism," Hoover's ideal. He admired and respected the efforts of individuals to excel in their fields and perhaps get rich, but he also believed that true American individualists would willingly cooperate to improve society and solve its problems. He believed that voluntary action by individuals could be a powerful force to improve the nation. Hoover's beliefs gained strength because his own life provided a good example.

"The Most Useful American"

In July 1923, Hoover traveled with President Warren Harding on a visit to Alaska. During the ship journey, Harding took Hoover aside. "If you knew of a great scandal in our administration," the president asked, "would you for the good of the country and the party expose it publicly or would you bury it?"

Hoover replied, "Publish it, and at least get credit for integrity on your side."

Only weeks later, Harding died of heart disease. The scandals of his administration were revealed only after his death, when Calvin Coolidge was president.

Hoover (right) served as secretary of commerce for more than five years under President Calvin Coolidge (left). The two men had very different personalities, and Hoover's advice sometimes irritated Coolidge.

Coolidge completed Harding's term and was elected in 1924 to a full term of his own. Hoover stayed on as secretary of commerce through the Coolidge years and conferred often with the president. The results were not always positive, however. Coolidge did not favor many of Hoover's pet projects. In fact, near the end of his term, Coolidge said, with a mixture of irritation and humor, "That man has been giving me advice every day for five years—all of it bad."

One of Hoover's most successful campaigns was to standardize thousands of parts for everyday products. He urged companies to agree on standard sizes for nuts and bolts, standard sizes for windows and doors when building new homes, and standard tire sizes for cars. Standardization helped lower the price of many items, including houses and cars. Critics blamed Hoover for doing away with old-fashioned individual workmanship, but he argued that lower prices gave people more choices and more chance to express their individualism.

In 1927 Hoover was thrown once again into relief work. That spring, the Mississippi River, swelled by the spring thaw and heavy rains, rose out of its banks and flooded hundreds of towns and villages. More than 1.5 million people in seven states lost their homes. Political leaders from the affected states clamored for government action, but President Coolidge opposed direct government grants, even for emergencies. In this case, Hoover came to the rescue. As he had done to conserve food during World War I, he appealed to the people of the United States to contribute generously to relieve the homeless and hungry. He helped the America Red Cross raise $16 million through a relief appeal that relied heavily on radio advertising. Then he arranged for indirect assistance from the state and federal governments. In all, he raised $36 million, and he helped deliver food, supplies, and financial aid promptly to those who needed it most. One flood victim said, "We think Hoover is the most useful American of his day."

An Opening at the White House

On August 2, 1927, Calvin Coolidge gave reporters a slip of paper that read, "I do not choose to run for president in nineteen twenty-eight." Almost immediately, Herbert Hoover became a favorite to gain the Republican nomination. Hoover-for-President clubs sprang up across the country, sponsored by friends, associates, and coworkers. The clubs brought attention to his administrative abilities and his scorn for traditional politicking. Hoover received a flood of telegrams urging him to announce his candidacy.

In June of 1928, at the Republican party's four-day nominating convention in Kansas City, Hoover won his party's nomination by a landslide, capturing 837 of 1,089 votes on the first ballot. The second highest vote-getter won only 74

In 1927, Hoover directed relief efforts for millions made homeless by the disastrous Mississippi River flood. Here he visits with young flood victims.

votes. With Hoover's approval, Senator Charles Curtis of Kansas was nominated to run for vice president.

Following the custom of the day, Hoover was not at the Kansas City convention. In his response accepting the nomination, he wrote of the United States, "It gave me, as it gives every boy and girl, a chance. It gave me schooling, independence of action, opportunity for service and honor. In no other land could a boy from a country village, without inheritance or influential friends, look forward with unbounded hope. My whole life has taught me what America means. I am indebted to my country beyond any human power to repay."

He kicked off his campaign August 11, at a huge rally in Stanford's football stadium. Standing before 70,000 cheering supporters, he called attention to the long "Coolidge prosperity," which he was hoping to continue. "We in America today are nearer to the final triumph over poverty than ever before in the history of any land." The speech was broadcast to a radio audience across the nation.

Governor Alfred E. Smith of New York won the Democratic nomination. Smith had been a progressive governor of New York, supporting laws that protected women and children in the workforce as well as other pro-labor legislation. The son of Irish immigrants and a Roman Catholic, he became a hero to millions of immigrants in New York, Chicago, and other big cities.

Hoover campaigns for the presidency in 1928.

Campaigning did not appeal to Hoover. He liked the way radio made it possible for him to give fewer speeches than had candidates in the past. He used it to deliver seven major addresses during the campaign. He spent a great deal of time preparing each of them himself. Hoover's campaign slogan, "A chicken in every pot and a car in every garage," made a reasonable promise in a country that was already prospering.

The two parties issued campaign *platforms* (lists of principles and promises) that were similar. Both pledged to reform the courts and the prison system; promote child welfare and better housing; improve the efficiency of the federal government; and conserve natural resources. Newspaper columnist Walter Lippmann said, "The two platforms contain no difference which would be called an issue."

One big difference between the parties was their views on *Prohibition*, the major social issue of the day. In 1919, campaigners against the evils of alcoholic beverages succeeded in passing the 18th Amendment to the Constitution, prohibiting the manufacture or sale of alcoholic beverages. In nearly ten years, the Prohibition laws had proved to be widely ineffective. They had created a profitable black market in illegal alcohol, often controlled by gangsters.

Al Smith was a leader of a growing campaign to *repeal* (or cancel) Prohibition. He had the enthusiastic support of his big-city followers. By contrast, the majority of Republicans, who lived in smaller towns and cities, wanted to keep

Prohibition in effect. The Hoovers had grown up among supporters of *temperance*, the movement to ban alcohol. Lou Hoover drank no alcohol and threatened to leave social gatherings where alcoholic drinks were served. She once gave away her husband's collection of rare wines. Hoover himself enjoyed an alcoholic drink in private, but he publicly approved the Republicans' support of Prohibition. He wrote that Prohibition was a "social and economic experiment, noble in motive" and that "alcohol is one of the curses of the human race." He was not convinced that Prohibition was a practical way to prevent alcohol abuse, but he pledged to uphold the law.

The other major issue in the campaign was religion. As the first Roman Catholic to run for president, Al Smith faced the suspicion and hostility of many Protestant Christians. Hoover never made a direct mention of Smith's religion, but local Republican campaigners did. They suggested that a Roman Catholic president would be required to follow Church policies and "take orders from the Pope." The religious issue hurt Smith not only with Republicans in the Midwest, but with loyal Democrats in the South.

By election day, it was clear that Hoover would be elected. Even so, the margin of his victory was surprising. He won 21.4 million votes to Smith's 15 million. In the electoral college, the Republican ticket carried 40 of the 48 states, winning 444 electoral votes to the Democrats' 87.

In his usual no-time-to-waste style, Hoover got to work even before he took office. To improve relations with American neighbors, he and Lou Hoover visited ten Latin American countries before the inauguration. Hoover established personal relationships with leaders, set up air travel policies, and encouraged exchange programs for teachers and students.

During a short Florida vacation in January 1929, Hoover told a newspaper editor, "I have no dread of the ordinary work of the presidency. What I do fear is the result of the exaggerated idea the people have conceived of me. They have a conviction that I am a sort of superman, that no problem is beyond my capacity."

Perhaps he sensed trouble on the horizon.

Chapter 4 Hoover at the Helm

A Strong Start

Hoover was inaugurated in March 1929 as the 31st president of the United States. The oath of office was administered by Chief Justice William Howard Taft, who had served as the 27th president. Like Hoover, Taft had spent most of his adult life in public service, but little in elective office. He had gained wide admiration for his abilities as an administrator and a mediator, yet his four years as president had been among the unhappiest of his life. President Hoover was about to have a similar experience.

Hoover entered office determined to work methodically toward his personal goals and those of his party. In many areas, he was continuing work he had begun years before. One example concerns the American Child Health Association (ACHA). Hoover had gained a deep and lasting concern for the welfare of children when he directed the food project for war-torn Belgium. When Hoover returned to the United States in 1919, he took an active role in improving child health and nutrition at home. In 1923, he helped form the ACHA and became its president. Even when he entered the White House, he continued as president of the organization.

The ACHA had learned that thousands of babies were dying each year because of sicknesses caused by unpasteurized milk. It persuaded local officials to pass laws requiring all milk to be disinfected by pasteurization, and infant deaths decreased. The organization took up programs to improve child nutrition, and it led a campaign to immunize children against smallpox and diphtheria, two dangerous diseases that caused many infant deaths. As president, Hoover extended ACHA programs to Puerto Rico and began efforts to improve child health in rural areas, especially in the South.

The president also took immediate steps to exercise better control over government lands. A week after he took office, he ended the sale of oil leases on public land and called for a review of existing oil leases. During his first three years as president, the National Park Service budget grew by almost 50 percent. New national parks were created, and 2 million acres (800,000 ha) of forests were turned into national preserves where development was restricted.

As president, Hoover launched another project he had long supported. He had campaigned when he was secretary of commerce to harness the power of the

Colorado River. He saw huge opportunities to control floods, provide water for cities and farm irrigation, and generate electricity. In 1922 he personally negotiated the Colorado River Compact with representatives of southwestern states and cities. The first project would be the construction of Boulder Dam in Black Canyon, on the border between Nevada and Arizona near Las Vegas. Congress approved the plan for the dam in December 1928, weeks after Hoover was elected. In 1931, construction of the dam finally began. It was completed in 1936. Water and electricity from the dam were soon flowing to cities as far away as San Diego and Los Angeles in California. In 1947, the dam was renamed Hoover Dam to honor Hoover's many contributions to the project.

All these achievements were soon overshadowed by the gradual and painful unraveling of the economy, which carried the nation into the depths of the Great Depression.

Wall Street and the Banks

On March 6, 1929, only two days after he became president, Hoover began consulting with leaders of the financial community. He was deeply concerned about the rapid increase of prices on the stock market. Old-fashioned investors bought *stocks* (shares of ownership in a private company) to collect small payments called dividends each year from the company's profits. Now a new kind of

Construction of Boulder Dam on the Colorado River, which began during Hoover's administration. It was later renamed Hoover Dam in his honor.

investor was buying stocks, hoping that they would quickly increase in value and could be sold for big profits. "Playing the market" seemed a way to get rich in a hurry. As the demand for popular stocks increased, their value went up and up. Hoover was especially worried because investors were now paying far more for stocks than they were really worth. Worse, many investors were buying stock with borrowed money. If the market suddenly went down, the investors wouldn't be able to pay their debts, and the nation's economy could be damaged.

Hoover discussed the problem with the Federal Reserve Board and with the president of the New York Stock Exchange. He urged them to limit the amount people could borrow to invest in stocks. They assured the president that such restrictions were not necessary and that there was no danger of a stock market collapse. Then in September 1929, stock prices began to decline. In October, they fell even faster.

On October 29, the market had its worst day in history, a day that became known as "Black Tuesday." By mid-November, stocks that had been worth $100 two months earlier were worth only $70. Lenders demanded that investors repay loans taken out for stock purchases. Many investors were forced to sell stocks at big losses in order to repay the loans. Some were forced to declare bankruptcy. A few, shamed by their failure, committed suicide.

A Bad Year

Hoover meets with baseball great Babe Ruth.

In 1930, baseball superstar Babe Ruth demanded a salary of $80,000 from the New York Yankees. Reporters pointed out that $80,000 was more than the president of the United States earned. "So what?" Ruth replied, "I had a better year than he did."

In 1929, only a small number of Americans actually invested in stocks, so the market crash did not affect the great majority of people. Business conditions and stock prices recovered after November. The president and financial experts assured the public that the stock market's drop was only temporary and predicted that prosperity would continue in 1930. Even so, President Hoover took action to make sure that the downturn did not cause further damage. He called meetings with important business leaders. They agreed not to reduce wages. Unions agreed not to ask for higher wages. State and local government officials agreed to speed up planned construction projects, which would offer increased employment. It appeared that Hoover's ability to gain voluntary cooperation might end the economic downturn.

In the fall of 1930, however, the stock market plunged again, and there were other worrisome signs. Confidence in banks was beginning to weaken, and many depositors withdrew their money. At the same time, many borrowers were unable to make payments on their loans. As a result, banks ran out of money and were forced to close. More than 600 closed in November and December 1930. Many depositors lost their life savings, and others were forced to close their businesses. Large manufacturers began laying off workers, and unemployment rose.

Many voters blamed the economic downturn on Hoover's Republican party. In the 1930 congressional elections, Democrats made large gains. They

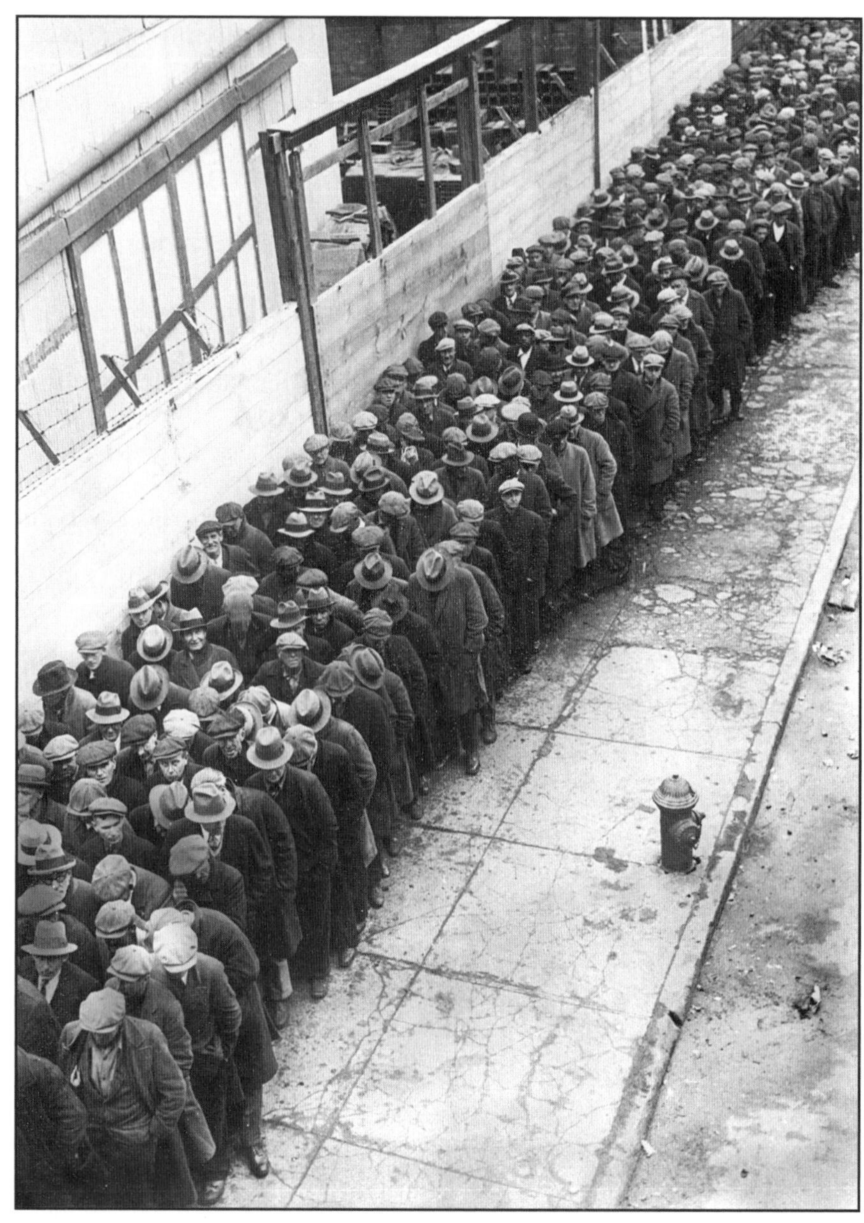

Homeless men line up to apply for shelter in New York during the Great Depression.

elected a majority in the House of Representatives and cut the Republican majority in the Senate to a single vote. Both parties were divided on what actions the government should take to bring back better times, but it was clear that Republicans would be punished if conditions got worse.

The Great Depression

In 1931, conditions did get worse. Other countries saw steep declines in stock prices and huge increases in unemployment. The world slid into the *Great Depression*, which brought unemployment, homelessness, and suffering to millions. In the United States, few could afford to buy new cars and other goods manufacturers were trying to sell. As a result, manufacturing companies laid off hundreds of thousands of workers. The stock market continued its plunge. Now stocks worth $100 in September 1929 were worth only $40.

World trade ground almost to a halt, and governments were no longer able to pay their debts to other governments. In June 1931, Hoover proposed giving European nations a one-year pause in the debts they owed to the United States. The plan gave European countries a chance to avoid complete bankruptcy, but conditions continued to worsen. Europeans with investments in the United States began withdrawing their money, putting even more pressure on U.S. banks.

During 1931, nearly 2,400 American banks closed their doors. As Hoover later wrote, "The bottom was fast dropping out of the economic world."

Assigning the Blame

Much of the public blamed the Depression on the three B's: bankers, brokers, and business. The most convenient target, however, was Hoover. Camps where the homeless lived were called "Hoovervilles." "Hoovercarts" were cars pulled by mules or horses because the owners could not afford gas. "Hooverflags" were empty pockets turned inside out. Humorist Will Rogers said, "If someone bit an apple and found a worm in it, Hoover would get the blame."

The voters who had elected Hoover by a huge margin in 1928 lost their admiration for him. When families could not pay their rent or put food on the table, they no longer responded to his calls for patriotism, cooperation, and common sense. Despite his broad knowledge of the economy and his history of feeding the hungry, Hoover seemed powerless to reassure his countrymen.

One cause of his failures lay in his own beliefs. He rejected calls for direct government assistance to the unemployed and homeless. Hoover supported charity from individuals or companies, but he feared that if the federal government paid unemployed workers, it would harm their sense of initiative and personal

A shantytown in Pittsburgh occupied by homeless people. Such settlements were known as Hoovervilles.

responsibility. Right or wrong, he stood by his conviction throughout his presidency. He was willing to provide federal jobs for unemployed workers, and he initiated several programs to construct public buildings, parks, and other improvements. Yet these programs were not enough to address the growing crisis.

Another cause for Hoover's failures was his inability to work productively with Congress. In 1931, seeking to protect American business from foreign competition, Congress passed the Hawley-Smoot Tariff Act, increasing *tariffs* (taxes on goods imported for sale) to their highest level in history. Economists warned that these high tariffs would only damage the country's trade with other nations and deepen economic distress. Hoover agreed with their argument, but the bill was very popular with Republican leaders, so he reluctantly signed it into law. Other countries soon passed similar high tariffs against U.S. goods, and U.S. foreign trade slowed to a trickle.

Finally, Hoover found it difficult to express his deep concern for the sufferings of ordinary people, and he could not find a rallying cry that would restore their confidence. In person or on the radio, his speeches were wooden and formal. An observer wrote, "One hand is kept in his pocket, usually jingling [coins or keys] placed there to ease his nerves. He has not a single gesture. . . . He reads—his chin down against his shirt front—rapidly and quite without expression."

On the Great Plains, bad economic times were made worse by severe drought and dust storms. This painting shows the ruined farmland that drove thousands of farmers to bankruptcy.

The Final Year

In January 1932, Hoover gave up his hopes for voluntary action to end the Depression. He asked Congress to form the Reconstruction Finance Corporation (RFC). "We used such emergency powers to win the war, we can use them to right the depression, the misery and suffering from which are equally great," he said. The RFC was authorized to issue $2 billion in federal funds as loans to banks. The loans were intended to end the growing list of bank closings and provide a source of loans to business and individuals. The RFC was praised by many in business as a major step toward ending the Depression. Others, however, complained that the RFC was simply a relief payment to rich bankers from a president who refused to offer relief payments to unemployed workers.

As the 1932 presidential election approached, Hoover faced increasing criticism from the Democrats, who saw a chance to regain the White House. A Democratic group was formed to call Hoover's virtues into question. They accused him of such far-fetched crimes as taking public money to build a personal fishing retreat and being involved in a kidnapping scandal. Mrs. Hoover said that if she believed half of what the Democrats said about her husband, she would not support him either! Hoover did his best to ignore his foes, saying, "I cannot take the time from my job to answer such stuff."

Unknown to the public, Hoover continued his long practice of accepting no pay—even as president. He quietly donated his salary each year to a private charity. He also did many other good deeds. In 1932, he helped two children from Detroit who had hitchhiked to Washington to get their father out of jail. Hoover listened to their story and helped gain their father's release. Yet he refused to let the story to be publicized.

Across the country, people's spirits sagged. Had the American dream collapsed? Popular newspaper columnist Will Rogers wrote, "There is not a man in the whole world today that people feel like actually knows what's the matter. . . . The case has simply got too big for the doctors, but the doctors haven't got big enough to admit it."

That summer, the Republican National Convention renominated Herbert Hoover for president. The delegates were not enthusiastic about their choice, but the party could not offer anyone more attractive. The Democrats nominated New York governor Franklin D. Roosevelt. A distant cousin of former president Theodore Roosevelt, Franklin had been a progressive governor who was widely admired for his winning smile and optimistic manner. Roosevelt promised a change in the White House, but remained vague about just what that change might entail.

The Bonus Army

In the summer of 1932, a ragtag "army" of demonstrators came to Washington. They were *veterans* of World War I (former members of the military during that war). They came to persuade the government to pay them a pension bond they had been granted after the war. Benefits were not scheduled to be paid until 1945, but the veterans argued that they needed the money now, when they were unemployed. They also argued that the money could help get the economy moving again.

The bond payment became known as the veteran bonus, and the marchers called themselves the Bonus Army. By June 1932, more than 10,000 were camping in or near Washington. Hoover's advisers urged him to keep the marchers out of Washington, but he refused. In fact, he arranged for them to be provided with clothing, beds, tents, medical supplies, kitchen equipment, and army food, free or at cost. He pointed out that the marchers had "been given every opportunity of free assembly, free speech and free petition to the Congress," but he refused to meet personally with them. Privately, he opposed the payment of the bonus, which would have cost the government more than $3 billion.

Many members of Congress were sympathetic to the veterans' cause, however. On June 16, the House of Representatives passed a bill granting full

The Bonus Army marchers rally on the steps of the Capitol in Washington in 1932.

payment. Two days later, with Hoover's support, the Senate voted overwhelmingly against the bill. Although Congress turned down the Bonus Army's demands, it did pay for free railroad tickets to send the demonstrators home.

About 6,000 of the marchers accepted the tickets and left Washington. The remaining marchers, some with their wives and children, continued to camp in vacant government buildings and in a shantytown on Anacostia Flats, a swampy area near the city. Weeks dragged by. During the day, they held rallies and demonstrated at the White House and the Capitol Building.

On July 29, Washington police ordered a group of marchers to leave an unused government building. When they refused, a riot occurred. Two policemen were injured, and one of the demonstrators was killed. Hoover ordered U.S. Army troops under the command of General Douglas MacArthur to force the marchers to leave the city and return to Anacostia. MacArthur followed the president's orders, but then went further. Using tear gas, he drove the Bonus Army stragglers out of their shantytown at Anacostia. Then he set fire to the tents and shacks there. One of MacArthur's assistants, Major Dwight Eisenhower, described the smoking ruins as "a pitiful scene."

Hoover was outraged that MacArthur had gone beyond his orders. Even so, he expressed no anger publicly and took full responsibility for the

The ruins of the Bonus Army's shantytown in Anacostia, destroyed by fire after the marchers were driven out by the U.S. Army.

MacArthur and Eisenhower

In the 1940s, General Douglas MacArthur became one of the heroes of U.S. action in World War II. He took a leading part in the war in the Pacific, and after Japan's surrender he served as military governor of Japan. He returned to active duty during the Korean War, but was relieved of his command in 1951 by President Harry Truman for refusing to obey an order.

Dwight Eisenhower also played a leading role in U.S. action during World War II, directing the Allied invasion of France in June 1944. In 1952, he ran for president on the Republican ticket and was elected, serving from 1953 to 1961.

tragedy. None of the demonstrators were killed, but news reports of the military action and photographs of the destruction caused shock and dismay across the country. When Franklin Roosevelt was told of the incident, he said, "This will elect me."

Chapter 5 Down and Out

Defeat

When Hoover returned to California in November 1932 to vote in the election, San Francisco crowds greeted him not with cheers, but with stink bombs. One heckler shouted, “Hey, Hoover, vote for Roosevelt and make it unanimous!”

Hoover did not expect to win the election, but he was shocked at how badly he lost. With 22.8 million votes to Hoover’s 15.8 million, Roosevelt won by an even larger margin than Hoover had gained in 1928. Roosevelt carried 42 states with 472 electoral votes to Hoover’s 6 states with 59 electoral votes.

During the four months between the election and Roosevelt’s inauguration in March 1933, the economy worsened rapidly. Even the largest and strongest banks in the country were near bankruptcy, and nearly a quarter of all U.S. workers were out of a job. During these grim months, Hoover worried that the economy might suffer from

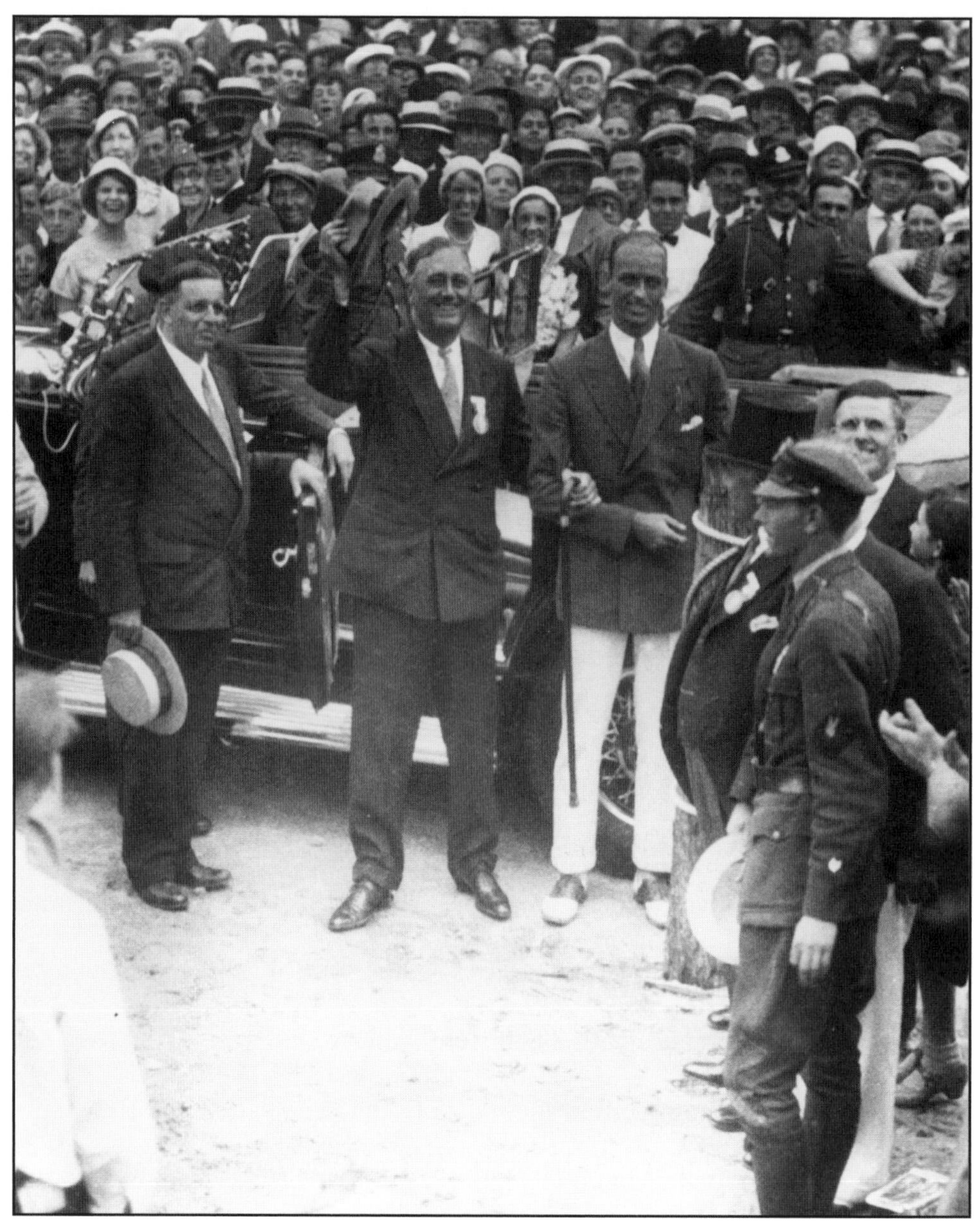

Franklin Roosevelt campaigns in New Hampshire during the 1932 campaign. He easily defeated Hoover in the November elections.

uncertainty during the transition. He met with the president-elect at the White House and tried to discuss his concerns with Roosevelt.

The meeting was a failure. Hoover seemed to dislike his younger and more popular successor and came to believe that he did not understand the situation. Roosevelt and his assistants resented Hoover's long lectures and scolding tone. The Democrats were unwilling to make any commitments to Hoover, afraid of being trapped into approving a Republican plan. Hoover was left to manage the crisis by himself until the inauguration on March 4. The unpleasant dealings between the two men also had a long-term effect for Hoover. During Roosevelt's twelve years as president, he was never asked for advice or assistance by the Democratic administration.

Roosevelt's first step after he took the oath of office was to reassure the American people. In the first paragraph of his inaugural address, he said,

> This is preeminently the time to speak the truth, the whole truth, frankly and boldly. Nor need we shrink from honestly facing conditions in our country today. This great Nation will endure as it has endured, will revive and will prosper. So, first of all, let me assert my firm belief that the only thing we have to fear is fear itself—nameless, unreasoning, unjustified terror which paralyzes needed efforts to convert retreat into advance.

Outgoing president Hoover shakes hands with incoming president Roosevelt on inauguration day in 1933.

Roosevelt soon mobilized the government to address many aspects of the depression. On March 6, he called a "bank holiday," closing all banks for a week while bank inspectors analyzed their operations and assessed their condition. Times did not improve rapidly, and the new government faced many of the same difficult obstacles as the old, but Roosevelt did restore a sense of optimism to many.

As for Hoover, he wrote that he felt a great sense of personal relief to be leaving the White House. "It was a release not alone from political pressures but from the routines of twelve to fourteen hours of work seven days a week." As his train pulled out of the Washington station, however, one observer said that tears rolled down Hoover's cheeks. His presidency, for which he had such ambitious plans, had ended in frustration and defeat.

Post-Election Activism

A year after Hoover left office, a fact-finding committee he had established early in his presidency finally released a two-volume, 1,600-page report, *Recent Social Trends in the United States*. It provided a detailed profile of the United States at the beginning of the Great Depression and offered suggestions on future economic policy. The report proved useful to the new administration, but it also recalled one of Roosevelt's criticisms of Hoover during the presidential campaign. Roosevelt complained that Hoover had "always shown a most disquieting desire to investigate everything and to appoint commissions and send out statistical inquiries on every conceivable subject under heaven."

Leaving Roosevelt to grapple with the Depression, Hoover moved back to Palo Alto. He turned some of his attention to mining, but he could not ignore events in the larger world. In fact, he read 30 newspapers daily! The Hoovers kept their Palo Alto home, but beginning in 1934, they lived most of each year at the Waldorf-Astoria Hotel in New York City, nearer the centers of national activity.

Hoover was pleased when Prohibition came to an end in 1933 with the passage of the 21st Amendment to the Constitution. He was much less pleased with many of the actions of Roosevelt's "New Deal." In Hoover's view, the new administration threatened precious American freedoms. He said, "You cannot extend the mastery of government over the daily life of a people without somewhere making it master of people's souls and thoughts."

World War II

In 1938 Hoover traveled to Europe, where he briefly met Adolf Hitler, the dictator who came to power by promising to lift Germany out of the Depression. Hoover was impressed by Hitler's intelligence, but noted the dictator's "furious anger." He said Hitler was "partly insane," and he warned that totalitarianism—dictatorship—was "on the march."

In 1939, under Hitler's leadership, Germany invaded Poland, and World War II began. The United States remained officially neutral, but President Roosevelt had close ties to Great Britain and was quietly providing assistance to the Allied nations opposing Germany. He was elected to a third term in 1940. On December 7, 1941, Japan (an ally of Germany) attacked Pearl Harbor, the U.S. naval base in Hawaii. The following day, the United States entered the war against Japan, Germany, and their allies.

Hoover had dreaded another terrible war, but supported U.S. actions after Pearl Harbor. During the war, Hoover suffered a sad personal loss. In January 1944, Lou Hoover died suddenly of a heart attack. For nearly 45 years she had shared his tumultuous life and been his most reliable supporter.

In April 1945, Franklin Roosevelt died in office, only weeks before the Allied forces defeated Germany in Europe. Vice President Harry Truman assumed the presidency. In August, Japan surrendered, and World War II came to an end. For the first time in twelve years, Herbert Hoover received an invitation to the White House. President Truman asked him to take charge of a program to provide food and other supplies to the people of Europe. Hoover was 71 years old, but he set off on a tour covering 35,000 miles (56,000 km) to survey the world's food needs. By the fall of 1946, he helped bring the situation under control. He urged that Germany not be punished economically after the war (as it had been after World War I). He supported the Marshall Plan, which provided billions of dollars to help rebuild Germany and its economy.

In 1947 President Truman asked Hoover to chair the Commission on Organization of the Executive Branch of the Government. Soon known as the Hoover Commission, it presented dozens of recommendations to streamline the government's executive branch. In 1953 he led a second commission for President Dwight D. Eisenhower. Many of the Hoover Commissions' recommendations were adopted. They helped the government run more efficiently, and they saved billions of dollars in government expenditures.

Ironically, Hoover's last act as a government official occurred in Belgium, where he began his years of public service in 1914. In 1958 he officially represented the United States at the opening of the World's Fair in Brussels, Belgium. In 1961, he was invited to attend the inauguration of President John F. Kennedy. Hoover had been a friend of the president's father, Joseph Kennedy, for many years. Hoover expressed his gratitude for the invitation, but decided not to attend because of his advanced age. Later that year he would be 87 years old.

Hoover (right) meets with President Harry Truman in 1945 to discuss relief efforts at the end of World War II in Europe.

Hoover speaks at his 80th birthday party in 1954.

In 1962 Hoover made his last public appearance in West Branch, Iowa. He visited his birthplace to dedicate the Herbert Hoover Presidential Library. By 1964, he was largely confined to his suite of rooms at the Waldorf-Astoria Hotel. Although he was deaf and nearly blind, he was still at work, writing a history of Communist influences on Western nations. On October 20 that year, after a brief illness, he died.

Hoover's funeral was held in St. Bartholomew's Episcopal Church, across the street from his apartment in the Waldorf-Astoria. At his request, the service seemed more a simple Quaker ceremony than an elaborate funeral for a president. He and Lou Henry Hoover were buried in West Branch, Iowa. Two simple granite stones mark their graves.

Chapter 6

The Hoover Legacy

An Unfortunate Presidency

Herbert Hoover entered the presidency in 1929 with high hopes. He had won election by a large majority and had the confidence of the nation. He was an expert in government administration and had a remarkable record as a problem solver. He looked forward to making government more effective in assisting growth and prosperity at home and in maintaining peace with other nations.

Only six months into his term, declining prices on the stock market and a slight business slowdown were the first signs of trouble. In the following years, the nation was engulfed by the Great Depression, the most serious economic reversal in its history. Hoover struggled to understand the causes of the Depression and to help bring it to an end, but nothing he did seemed to have much effect. Four years after his election by a large majority, he was turned out of office by an even larger majority.

President Herbert Hoover.

Presidents and Panics

Hoover was not the first or the last president whose term of office was ruined by an economic depression. Only months after Martin Van Buren was elected in 1837, a severe panic or depression struck the country. Van Buren was unable to bring it to an end, and four years later, he lost his bid for re-election. A panic in 1893 cast a cloud over the presidency of Grover Cleveland, and he left office as one of the most unpopular presidents in history. More recently, President George H. W. Bush failed to gain re-election in 1992 after a drop in the stock market and a rise in unemployment.

☆☆☆

It seems clear to historians that Hoover did not cause the depression, but it began and reached one of its lowest points during his term of office. In addition, people at the time believed that he took no effective actions to address individual suffering or to end the downward spiral of the economy. Sadly, the man who had helped feed millions in Europe during World War I could not find a way to feed millions of hungry Americans during his presidency. As a result, Hoover's presidency was among the unhappiest and least successful in history.

Strengths and Weaknesses

In many ways, Hoover came to the presidency better prepared than almost any candidate up to that time. He had demonstrated great abilities both in business and in government. He was a talented administrator famous for his ability to "get things done." When he ran for president, he had served for eight years in the cabinet as secretary of commerce and had advised two earlier presidents on a wide range of issues.

After he became president, however, Hoover revealed some of his weaknesses. Most important, he proved ineffective as a political leader. Unlike most earlier presidents, he had never been elected to office, either as a legislator or as a governor. He found it difficult to negotiate with powerful leaders in Congress to hammer out legislation that would gain broad political support. Even representatives and senators in his own Republican party often opposed his recommendations and helped pass measures he disapproved of.

Hoover's other major weakness was revealed as the crisis of the Great Depression deepened. Even though he was personally compassionate and generous, he seemed unable to communicate this to the public in his speeches and writings. He spent endless hours negotiating with bankers and business leaders, but never succeeded in rallying the general public to his views. As the Depression deepened and suffering increased, Hoover seemed defensive and defeated.

Accomplishments

At one point during World War I, Hoover wrote about his own life: "When all is said and done, accomplishment is all that counts." What did Hoover accomplish?

Despite his difficult term as president, Herbert Hoover left an impressive record of achievement.

As the leader of relief efforts during World War I and after both world wars, he helped save millions from starvation. As food administrator for the United States during World War I, he made a major contribution to bringing the war to a successful conclusion, persuading Americans to save food for shipment to the war zones.

At home, his long campaign for children's health helped create modern pure food laws and immunization programs that allowed millions of children to survive and become healthy adults. After he left the presidency, he took an active role in supporting the Boys Club of America and helped establish more than 500 new clubs. Today the Boys and Girls Clubs of America have more than 3.5 million members.

Hoover also took a leading role in encouraging economic growth in the United States. His longtime support of the Colorado River Project led to the construction of Hoover Dam. Water and power from the project helped California become the most populous state in the nation and greatly expanded the national economy.

Long after leaving the presidency, Hoover made a major contribution to more effective government. Working with Democratic president Harry Truman

The Hoover Institution

The terrible suffering caused by World War I gave Hoover a deep concern about the possibility of future wars. In 1919 he contributed $50,000 to establish the Hoover War Institution at Stanford University to preserve documents about the war and study ways of preventing future conflicts.

Hoover continued his active interest in the institution for the rest of his life. Today it is known as the Hoover Institution on War, Revolution, and Peace. It occupies the Hoover Tower, a landmark on the Stanford campus, and the Lou Henry Hoover Building. The institution offers scholars opportunities to study issues relating to war and peace and the preservation of American values and ideals.

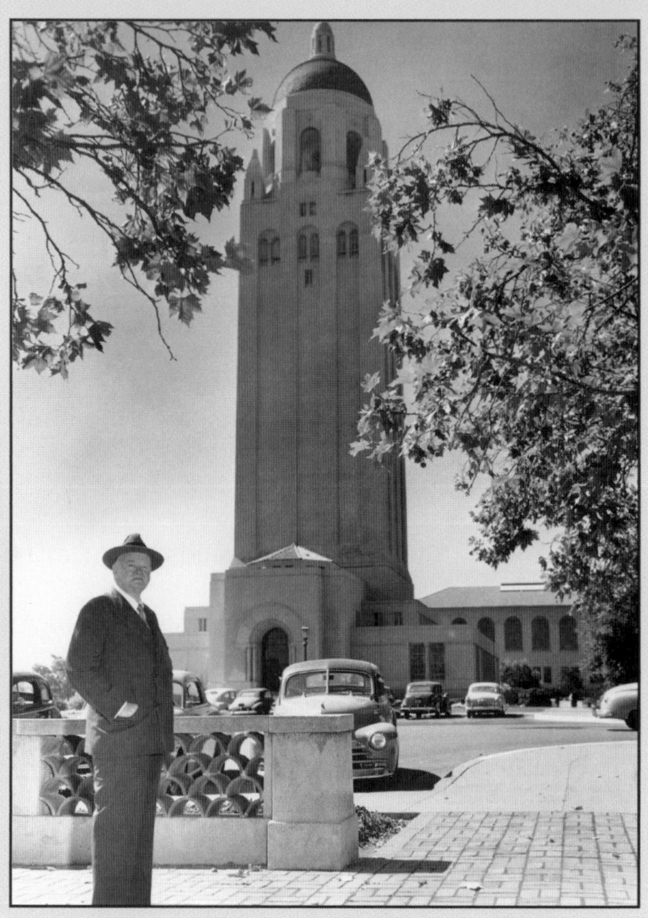

Hoover stands outside the Hoover Tower, part of the Hoover Institution at Stanford University.

and Republican Dwight Eisenhower, two Hoover Commissions helped reorganize the federal government, reducing waste and improving its effectiveness.

Hoover also helped define and defend the main values of the modern Republican party. He believed that every person should have the chance to succeed as an individual, but he insisted that individuals had an obligation to help in their communities. He was an active leader in government, but he strongly defended the contributions of free enterprise.

Final Accounting

Herbert Hoover served as president during four of the most disastrous years in the nation's history. Although he seemed well prepared to be president, he struggled with little success against the huge forces that caused the Great Depression. Perhaps a different president with different strengths might have had more success in leading the country during those difficult years. Yet Hoover's experience suggests that all the powers of a president are sometimes not enough to control world events.

Hoover is remembered as a disappointing president, but he is also remembered as a man who made important contributions to the United States and the world over 50 years of public service. He saved millions from starvation, fought

Herbert and Lou Hoover are buried on the gently rolling prairie in West Branch, Iowa.

to protect and encourage the young, helped make the nation's government more effective and efficient, and promoted the study of peace and an end to war. It is a record any person would be proud of.

PRESIDENTIAL

Fast Facts

Herbert Hoover

Birth:	August 10, 1874
Birthplace:	West Branch, Iowa
Parents:	Jesse Hoover and Hulda Minthorn Hoover
Brothers & Sisters:	Theodore Jesse (Tad) (1871–1955)
	Mary Blanche (May) (1876–1953)
Education:	Stanford University, Palo Alto, California; graduated 1895
Occupation:	Engineer, executive
Marriage:	To Lou Henry, February 10, 1899
Children:	(see First Lady Fast Facts at right)
Political Party:	Republican
Government Service:	1917–1919 U.S. Food Administrator (during World War I)
	1919–1921 Director, American Relief Administration
	1921–1928 U.S. Secretary of Commerce
	1929–1933 31st President of the United States
	1947–1948 Director of Commission on Organization of the Executive Branch of the Government (first Hoover Commission)
	1953–1954 Director of second Hoover Commission
His Vice President:	Charles Curtis
Major Actions as President:	1929 Signed Agricultural Marketing Act to help stabilize farm prices
	1930 Gained pledges from business not to reduce wages and from local governments to speed up public works projects
	1931 Signed moratorium on European payment of debts to the U.S.
	1932 Reconstruction Finance Corporation made loans to distressed banks
	1933 Called in military to move Bonus Army from Washington
Death:	October 20, 1964
Age at Death:	90
Burial Place:	Herbert Hoover National Historic Site, West Branch, Iowa

First Lady

Fast Facts

Lou Henry Hoover

Birth:	March 29, 1874
Birthplace:	Waterloo, Iowa
Parents:	Charles D. Henry and Florence Weed Henry
Brothers & Sisters:	Jean (1882–?)
Education:	Stanford University, Palo Alto, California; graduated 1898
Marriage:	To Herbert Hoover, February 10, 1899
Children:	Herbert Clark Junior (1903–1969)
	Allan Henry (1907–1993)
Death:	January 7, 1944
Age at Death:	69
Burial Place:	Herbert Hoover National Historic Site, West Branch, Iowa

Timeline

1874 Herbert Clark Hoover born to Jesse and Hulda Hoover in West Branch, Iowa, August 10

1880 Hoover's father dies

1884 Hoover's mother dies

1885 Hoover moves to Oregon to live with his aunt and uncle, Laura and John Minthorn

1891 Enrolls in first class at Stanford University, Palo Alto, California

1903 Herbert Clark Hoover Junior born in London

1907 Allan Henry Hoover born in London

1909 Hoover publishes *Principles of Mining*; retires from Bewick, Moreing; returns to California

1914 Helps Americans stranded by World War I; becomes chairman of the Commission for Relief in Belgium

1917 U.S. enters World War I; Hoover becomes U.S. Food Administrator

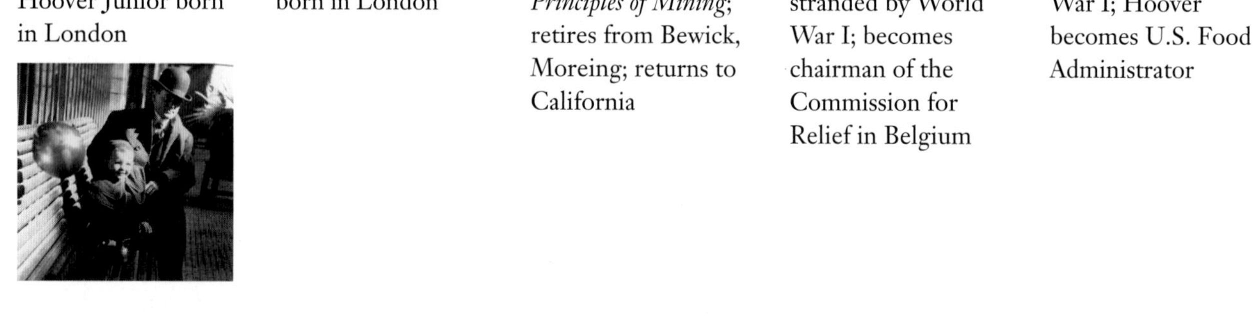

1929 Becomes 31st president, March; U.S. stock market crashes, October

1931 Signs moratorium on payment of war debts to U.S. by European nations

1932 Runs for re-election, loses to Democrat Franklin D. Roosevelt

1936 Serves as chairman of Boys Club of America and helps establish 500 new clubs

1944 Lou Henry Hoover dies

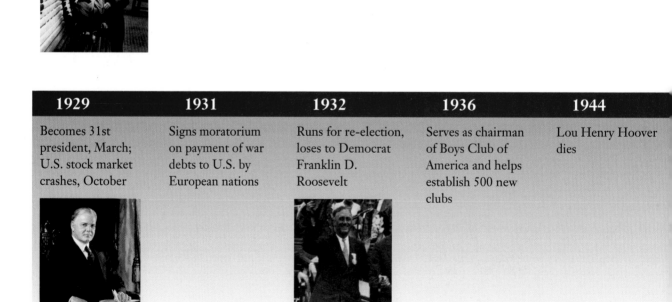

1895

Graduates from Stanford University with B.A. in geology; begins mining career

1897

Hired by British mining firm of Bewick, Moreing and Company, works in Australia

1899

Marries Lou Henry in Monterey, California

1899

Begins mining work in China for Bewick, Moreing

1901

Becomes partner in Bewick, Moreing; moves to London

1919

Establishes the Hoover Institution at Stanford University

1921

Becomes U.S. secretary of commerce, serves until 1928

1923

Becomes president of American Child Health Association, serves until 1935

1927

Administers flood relief to victims of Mississippi River flood

1928

Receives Republican nomination for president, June; is elected, November

1947

Leads the Hoover Commission on reorganizing government, under President Truman

1953

Directs second Hoover Commission on reorganization, under President Eisenhower

1962

Dedicates the Hoover Presidential Library and Museum in West Branch, Iowa

1964

Dies at age 90 in New York City, October 20

Glossary

armistice: an agreement to stop fighting while a peace treaty is negotiated

geology: the scientific study of the earth and its formation

Great Depression: a worldwide downturn in business and employment which began about 1931 and continued in the United States until about 1939

labor: persons who work in factories or other large businesses

management: persons who own or manage factories or other large businesses

platform: a political party's list of principles and promises, usually agreed on before an election

Prohibition: the laws passed under the 18th Amendment to the U.S. Constitution, forbidding the manufacture or sale of alcoholic drinks

rationing: limitation of the amount of certain items that families or individuals may buy (usually imposed during wartime or other national emergency)

repeal: to cancel a law or regulation that is already in effect; the United States repealed Prohibition in 1933

secretary of commerce: in the U.S. government, the cabinet officer whose role is to encourage U.S. trade at home and abroad

stock: shares of ownership in a private corporation

tariff: a tax on goods imported into a country for sale

temperance: a movement in the United States to end alcohol abuse; most temperance supporters campaigned to prohibit the manufacture or sale of alcoholic drinks

union: a labor organization that bargains with management to improve pay, benefits, and working conditions for its members

veterans: those who have performed military service

Further Reading

Colbert, Nancy A. *Lou Henry Hoover: The Duty to Service*. Greensboro, NC: Morgan Reynolds, 1998.

Souter, Gerry, and Janet Souter. *Herbert Hoover: Our Thirty-first President*. Chanhassen, MN: Child's World, 2001.

Teitelbaum, Michael S. *Herbert Hoover*. Minneapolis, MN: Compass Point Books, 2002.

MORE ADVANCED READING

Fausold, Martin L. *The Presidency of Herbert C. Hoover*. Lawrence: University of Kansas Press, 1994.

Steinbeck, John. *The Grapes of Wrath*. New York: Penguin Books, 2002 (reprint).

Walch, Timothy. *Uncommon Americans: The Lives and Legacies of Herbert and Lou Henry Hoover*. Westport, CT: Praeger Publishers, 2003.

Wilson, Joan Hoff. *Herbert Hoover: Forgotten Progressive*. Long Grove, IL: Waveland Press, 1992.

Places to Visit

The Herbert Hoover Presidential Library-Museum
210 Parkside Drive
West Branch, IA 52358
(319) 643-5301
http://hoover.archives.gov/visiting/index.html

The 186-acre (74 ha) site includes the Hoover Presidential Library-Museum and the Hoover Birthplace Cottage. Hoover and his wife Lou Henry Hoover are buried here.

Hoover Dam
Boulder City, NV
http://www.usbr.gov/lc/hooverdam

The dam is located on the Colorado River, about 30 miles (48 km) southeast of Las Vegas, Nevada. Nearly a million visitors tour the dam each year.

The Hoover Institution on War, Revolution, and Peace
Stanford University
Stanford, CA 94305-6010
(650) 723-1754; (877) 466-8374
http://www-hoover.stanford.edu/

This complex was founded as the Hoover Institution Archives in 1919. It now occupies three buildings on the campus of Stanford, including the landmark Hoover Tower.

The Hoover-Minthorn House Museum
115 South River Street
Newberg, OR 97132
(503) 538-629

Hoover lived here with his aunt and uncle, Laura and John Minthorn, and their daughters from 1885 to 1891.

Online Sites of Interest

★ **The Herbert Hoover Presidential Library-Museum**

http://hoover.archives.gov/

Provides extensive information about Hoover, his presidency, research materials, and related sites.

★ **Hoover Dam**

http://www.usbr.gov/lc/hooverdam

Describes the history of the dam, provides interesting facts, answers frequently asked questions, gives directions to the dam, and suggests things to see and do there.

★ **The Hoover Institution**

http://www.hoover.org

Describes the history of the institution and the resources it provides.

★ **The American President**

http://www.americanpresident.org/history/herberthoover/

A detailed and informative biography of Hoover provides background information on his early life, family, career, and presidency. This site provides biographies of all the presidents.

★ **The American Presidency**

http://gi.grolier.com/presidents/

Offers information on the presidents at several different reading levels, presidential portraits, and information about presidential elections.

★ **Presidents of the United States**

http://www.ipl.org/div/potus/hchoover.html

Provides facts about Hoover and links to sites of special interest to children and teen researchers.

★ **National First Ladies' Library**

http://www.firstladies.org

Contains photos and articles about the contributions of first ladies and other important women in American history.

Table of Presidents

	1. George Washington	2. John Adams	3. Thomas Jefferson	4. James Madison
Took office	Apr 30 1789	Mar 4 1797	Mar 4 1801	Mar 4 1809
Left office	Mar 3 1797	Mar 3 1801	Mar 3 1809	Mar 3 1817
Birthplace	Westmoreland Co, VA	Braintree, MA	Shadwell, VA	Port Conway, VA
Birth date	Feb 22 1732	Oct 20 1735	Apr 13 1743	Mar 16 1751
Death date	Dec 14 1799	July 4 1826	July 4 1826	June 28 1836

	9. William H. Harrison	10. John Tyler	11. James K. Polk	12. Zachary Taylor
Took office	Mar 4 1841	Apr 6 1841	Mar 4 1845	Mar 5 1849
Left office	**Apr 4 1841•**	Mar 3 1845	Mar 3 1849	**July 9 1850•**
Birthplace	Berkeley, VA	Greenway, VA	Mecklenburg Co, NC	Barboursville, VA
Birth date	Feb 9 1773	Mar 29 1790	Nov 2 1795	Nov 24 1784
Death date	Apr 4 1841	Jan 18 1862	June 15 1849	July 9 1850

	17. Andrew Johnson	18. Ulysses S. Grant	19. Rutherford B. Hayes	20. James A. Garfield
Took office	Apr 15 1865	Mar 4 1869	Mar 5 1877	Mar 4 1881
Left office	Mar 3 1869	Mar 3 1877	Mar 3 1881	**Sept 19 1881•**
Birthplace	Raleigh, NC	Point Pleasant, OH	Delaware, OH	Orange, OH
Birth date	Dec 29 1808	Apr 27 1822	Oct 4 1822	Nov 19 1831
Death date	July 31 1875	July 23 1885	Jan 17 1893	Sept 19 1881

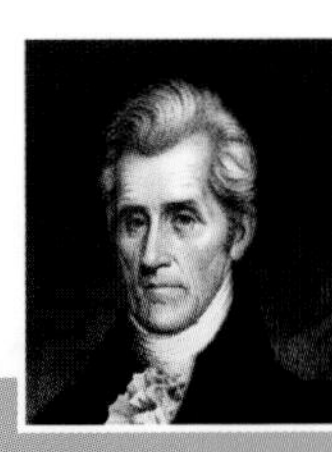

5. James Monroe	6. John Quincy Adams	7. Andrew Jackson	8. Martin Van Buren
Mar 4 1817	Mar 4 1825	Mar 4 1829	Mar 4 1837
Mar 3 1825	Mar 3 1829	Mar 3 1837	Mar 3 1841
Westmoreland Co,VA	Braintree, MA	The Waxhaws, SC	Kinderhook, NY
Apr 28 1758	July 11 1767	Mar 15 1767	Dec 5 1782
July 4 1831	Feb 23 1848	June 8 1845	July 24 1862

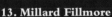

13. Millard Fillmore	14. Franklin Pierce	15. James Buchanan	16. Abraham Lincoln
July 9 1850	Mar 4 1853	Mar 4 1857	Mar 4 1861
Mar 3 1853	Mar 3 1857	Mar 3 1861	**Apr 15 1865•**
Locke Township, NY	Hillsborough, NH	Cove Gap, PA	Hardin Co, KY
Jan 7 1800	Nov 23 1804	Apr 23 1791	Feb 12 1809
Mar 8 1874	Oct 8 1869	June 1 1868	Apr 15 1865

21. Chester A. Arthur	22. Grover Cleveland	23. Benjamin Harrison	24. Grover Cleveland
Sept 19 1881	Mar 4 1885	Mar 4 1889	Mar 4 1893
Mar 3 1885	Mar 3 1889	Mar 3 1893	Mar 3 1897
Fairfield,VT	Caldwell, NJ	North Bend, OH	Caldwell, NJ
Oct 5 1829	Mar 18 1837	Aug 20 1833	Mar 18 1837
Nov 18 1886	June 24 1908	Mar 13 1901	June 24 1908

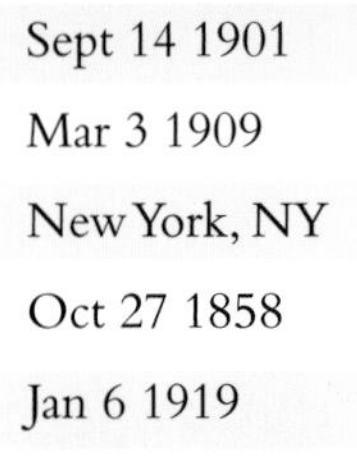

	25. William McKinley	26. Theodore Roosevelt	27. William H. Taft	28. Woodrow Wilson
Took office	Mar 4 1897	Sept 14 1901	Mar 4 1909	Mar 4 1913
Left office	**Sept 14 1901•**	Mar 3 1909	Mar 3 1913	Mar 3 1921
Birthplace	Niles, OH	New York, NY	Cincinnati, OH	Staunton, VA
Birth date	Jan 29 1843	Oct 27 1858	Sept 15 1857	Dec 28 1856
Death date	Sept 14 1901	Jan 6 1919	Mar 8 1930	Feb 3 1924

	33. Harry S. Truman	34. Dwight D. Eisenhower	35. John F. Kennedy	36. Lyndon B. Johnson
Took office	Apr 12 1945	Jan 20 1953	Jan 20 1961	Nov 22 1963
Left office	Jan 20 1953	Jan 20 1961	**Nov 22 1963•**	Jan 20 1969
Birthplace	Lamar, MO	Denison, TX	Brookline, MA	Johnson City, TX
Birth date	May 8 1884	Oct 14 1890	May 29 1917	Aug 27 1908
Death date	Dec 26 1972	Mar 28 1969	Nov 22 1963	Jan 22 1973

	41. George Bush	42. Bill Clinton	43. George W. Bush
Took office	Jan 20 1989	Jan 20 1993	Jan 20 2001
Left office	Jan 20 1993	Jan 20 2001	—
Birthplace	Milton, MA	Hope, AR	New Haven, CT
Birth date	June 12 1924	Aug 19 1946	July 6 1946
Death date	—	—	—

29. Warren G. Harding	30. Calvin Coolidge	31. Herbert Hoover	32. Franklin D. Roosevelt
Mar 4 1921	Aug 2 1923	Mar 4 1929	Mar 4 1933
Aug 2 1923•	Mar 3 1929	Mar 3 1933	**Apr 12 1945•**
Blooming Grove, OH	Plymouth, VT	West Branch, IA	Hyde Park, NY
Nov 21 1865	July 4 1872	Aug 10 1874	Jan 30 1882
Aug 2 1923	Jan 5 1933	Oct 20 1964	Apr 12 1945

37. Richard M. Nixon	38. Gerald R. Ford	39. Jimmy Carter	40. Ronald Reagan
Jan 20 1969	Aug 9 1974	Jan 20 1977	Jan 20 1981
Aug 9 1974★	Jan 20 1977	Jan 20 1981	Jan 20 1989
Yorba Linda, CA	Omaha, NE	Plains, GA	Tampico, IL
Jan 9 1913	July 14 1913	Oct 1 1924	Feb 6 1911
Apr 22 1994	—	—	June 5 2004

• Indicates the president died while in office.

★ Richard Nixon resigned before his term expired.

Index

Page numbers in *italics* indicate illustrations.

About the Author

Martha E. Kendall earned a B.A. at the University of Michigan and an M.A. in English at Stanford University, Herbert Hoover's alma mater. She also holds a master's degree in social science from San Jose State University. She has written a dozen books for children and young adults, including *Steve Wozniak, Inventor of the Apple Computer*, and *Failure Is Impossible: The History of American Women's Rights*.

When Martha Kendall was a child, her parents urged her not to let food go to waste. They told her to "have a Hoover" by eating everything on her plate. She never forgot the expression. Kendall regularly plays in bluegrass and string ensembles, and she has performed at the Hoover mansion on the Stanford campus. She lives with her husband, Joe Weed, and their two children in the Santa Cruz Mountains of northern California.